Englisch-Stars 3

Für Profis

Erarbeitet von

Jasmin Brune
Daniela Elsner
Stefanie Gleixner-Weyrauch
Marion Lugauer
Sabine Schwarz

Illustriert von
Barbara Jung
Thilo Pustlauk
Wilfried Poll

Cornelsen

Inhalt

 Comic

Hello Sally and Koala

HOP HOP

Hey, stop that!

Hi. My name is Koala.

Oh sorry. Hi. I'm Sally the kangaroo. What's your name?

Nice to meet you, Sally.

Nice to meet you, Koala.

Sorry, I'm so tired. I'm going back to sleep. Goodbye, Sally.

Bye bye Koala. Sleep well.

Draw lines.

What's your name?	Nett, dich kennenzulernen.
Nice to meet you.	Wie heiβt du?
Hi.	Ich heiβe …
Bye bye.	Hallo.
My name is …	Tschüss.

Verbinde, was zusammengehört.

Comic

I like colours

What a grey day today. I don't like grey.

I've got an idea!

The sky is blue.

The sun is yellow.

The tree is green and brown.

The flowers are red, orange and pink.

What a colourful day. I like colours. And I like me.

1. True or false? Tick ✓.

	true	false
The sky is green.	○	○
Sally likes grey.	○	○
The sun is yellow.	○	○
The flowers are pink, red and orange.	○	○
Sally is black.	○	○

Richtig oder falsch? Mache einen Haken.

2. Write.

Schau dir nochmal den Comic an und schreibe die Farben der Dinge auf. Und Sally?

What colour is the ? The ____________ is ____________.

What colour is the ? The ____________ is ____________.

What colour is the ? The ____________ is ____________ and ____________.

What colour are the ? The ____________ are ____________, ____________ and ____________.

What colour is Sally? ____

____.

black blue brown
green grey orange
pink purple
red white yellow

colourful – bunt
day – Tag
flowers – Blumen
idea – Idee
sky – Himmel
sun – Sonne
tree – Baum

3. Read. Write in the correct colour.

green	______	black	______
red	______	grey	______
blue	______	purple	______
pink	______	brown	______
orange	______	yellow	______

Schreibe die Wörter in der richtigen Farbe.

4. Colour the picture. Write.

The sky is ______.

The sun is ______.

The tree is ______.

The flowers are ______.

Sally is ______.

Male das Bild an und vervollständige die Sätze.

Which colour do you like best?

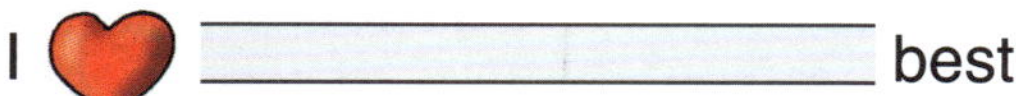

I ❤ ______ best.

Comic

The number code

SNIFF
SNIFF
SCHOOL
Hey Tim, what's the matter?
I've got a new lock for my bike. But I don't remember the number code.
Try your birthday...
1, 5, 1, 2... No, that's not the correct number code.
Try the first four numbers of your telephone number.
3, 9, 8, 2... No, that's not the correct number code.
Try even numbers only.
2, 4, 6, 8... No, that's not the correct number code.
I'm such an idiot. I have **absolutely no idea.**
Zero,
zero,
zero idea...
CLICK
Yeah... That's it... Zero, zero, zero, zero!

1. True or false? Tick ✓.

	true	false
Tim has got a new bike.	○	○
Tim doesn't remember his number code.	○	○
Tim's birthday is in December.	○	○
Tim's telephone number starts with 3.	○	○
The correct number code is 9999.	○	○

2. Which tips do the children give Tim? Tick ✓.

Welche Ratschläge geben die Kinder Tim? Mache Haken.

Try…

- ☐ your birthday.
- ☐ the first four numbers of your telephone number.
- ☐ your mum's birthday.
- ☐ odd numbers.
- ☐ even numbers.

one two three four five six seven eight nine ten eleven twelve

even numbers – gerade Zahlen

idea – Idee

lock – Schloss

number code – Zahlencode

odd numbers – ungerade Zahlen

to try – versuchen

zero – Null

That's it! – Das ist es!

What's the matter – Was ist los?

3. Read and write the numbers.

Write these numbers in the correct order:
seven, two, twelve, nine, ten, four, six, eight

Alle geraden Zahlen (*even numbers*) kannst du durch zwei teilen. Ungerade Zahlen (*odd numbers*) nicht.

Write down all even numbers from 1 – 12:

two

Write down all odd numbers from 1 – 12:

one

4. Colour.

one	= blue
two	= green
three	= yellow
four	= pink
five	= brown
six	= grey
seven	= red
eight	= orange
nine	= purple
ten	= red
eleven	= black
twelve	= white

Comic

Where is the chalk?

Where is my chalk? Can you help me find it, please?

Little Red Riding Hood, have you got my chalk?

Sorry, no, I haven't. I've just got a book, a ruler, a glue stick, a cake and some flowers.

Frog Prince, have you got my chalk?

Sorry, no, I haven't. I've just got a pair of scissors, a rubber, a pen and a golden ball.

Cinderella, have you got my chalk?

Sorry, no, I haven't. I've just got a pencil case, a green pencil, a folder and a shoe.

Sleeping Beauty, have you got my chalk?

Sorry, no, I haven't. I've just got a red pencil, a ruler, a rubber and a spindle.

Sorry, I like to eat chalk.

1. What belongs together? Colour.

Der Wolf und die sieben Geißlein

Aschenputtel

Dornröschen

Cinderella

The Frog Prince

Little Red Riding Hood

Sleeping Beauty

Male die drei Kästen, die jeweils zusammengehören, in derselben Farbe aus.

Rotkäppchen

The wolf and the seven young kids

Froschkönig

board book chair chalk computer desk folder
glue stick pen pencil pencil case pencil sharpener
rubber ruler scissors schoolbag pupil school uniform
teacher art maths music science sports subject

cake – Kuchen
flowers – Blumen
golden ball – goldene Kugel

shoe – Schuh
spindle – Spindel

Schau dir den Comic nochmal an und schreibe auf, welche Schulsachen die Märchenfiguren jeweils haben.

2. What school things have they got? Write.

Little Red Riding Hood has got a ruler ____________________

____.

Cinderella has got a ______________________________

____.

The Frog Prince has got a __________________________

____.

Sleeping Beauty has got a __________________________

____.

3. Read and colour the school things.

Lies und male die Schulsachen in den richtigen Farben aus.

My schoolbag is green and my pencil case is orange.
My scissors are black and my rubber is blue.
My glue stick is red.
My book is brown and the ruler is yellow.
My pencils are green, pink, black and purple.

4. Look and write.

The ______________ is **under** the basket.

The ______________ is **on** the basket.

The ______________ is **in** the basket.

Lies den Text und setze die Wörter ein.

5. Read and fill in the gaps.

ends **sports** **friends** **morning**

Hello, my ______ is Nick. I go to Westminster ______ .
I'm in ______ 3c. My ______ is Mrs Green. My school ______
is blue and white. School ______ at 9 o'clock in the morning
and ______ at 4 o'clock in the afternoon. Every ______ we have
assembly. At 12.30 it's lunchtime. I eat at school with my ______ .
I like ______ and music best.

teacher **uniform** **school** **starts** **name** **class**

Now it's your turn. Fill in.

Hello, my name is ______________. I go to ______________ school.

I'm in class ______________. My teacher is Mr. / Mrs. ______________.

School starts at ______________ and ends at ______________.

I like ______________________.

Comic

Let's be happy!

At night Tommy doesn't sleep in his bed …
… He flies into space in his pot and looks for new planets.
Hello, I'm Tommy. Are you all right?
I'm so sad. I'm so lonely. I haven't got any friends.
PLASH
Go away! I'm angry! Nobody likes me. I haven't got any friends.
GRRRR
Why are you so tired?
It's so boring, I haven't got any friends.
ZZZ
ZZZZZ
ZZZZ
I've got an idea!
PLEASE COME TO MY PLANET PARTY
We are all happy now. We are all friends.

1. True or false? Tick ✓.

	true	false
At night Tommy sleeps in his pot.	○	○
Tommy is flying in his pot.	○	○
The green planet is angry.	○	○
The red planet is angry.	○	○
The blue planet is tired.	○	○
All the planets are sad in the end.	○	○
The planets are having a birthday party.	○	○

Die Mehrzahl von Nomen bildet man, indem man ein -s an das Wort hängt, z.B.
1 arm – 2 arms, 1 leg – 2 legs.
Es gibt aber auch unregelmäßige Nomen, z.B.
1 foot – 2 feet, 1 tooth – 2 teeth.

arm ear eye
foot – feet hand
leg mouth nose
tooth – teeth
angry happy
hungry sad
scared tired

boring – langweilig
to fly – fliegen
idea – Idee
lonely – einsam
night – Nacht
pot – Topf
to sleep – schlafen

space – Weltall
planet – Planet
Go away! – Geh weg!

Schau dir die Planeten genau an und beschreibe sie.

2. Describe the planets. Write.

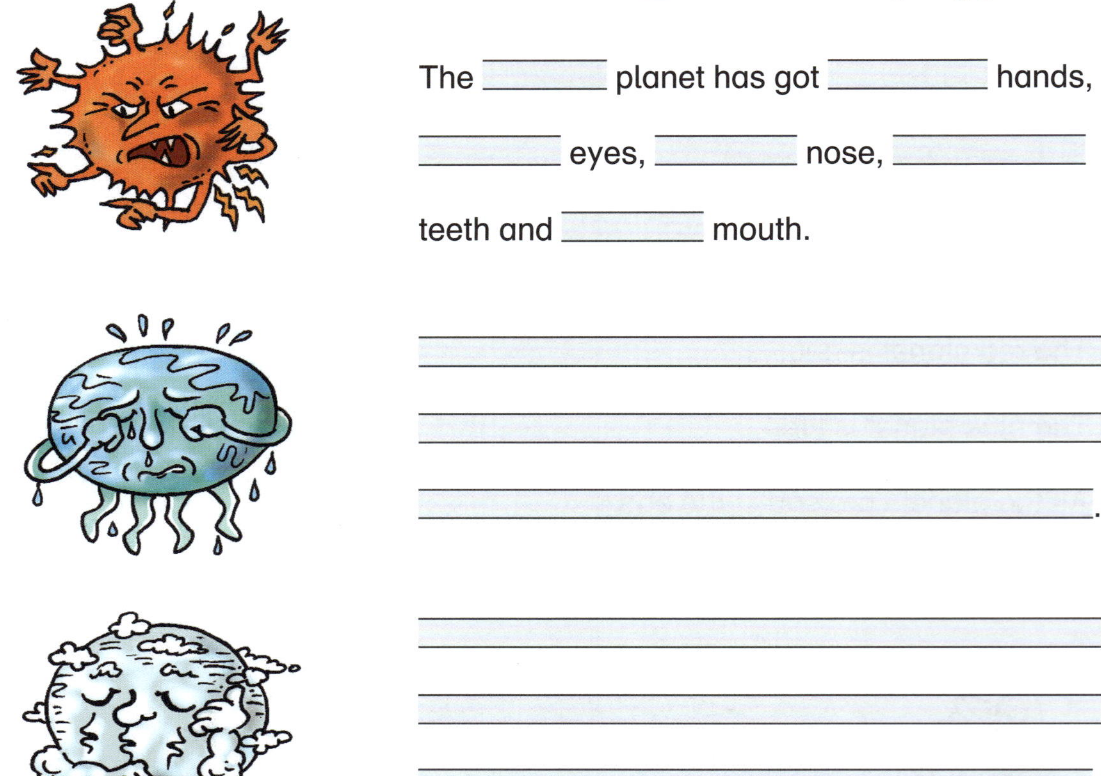

The ________ planet has got ________ hands,

________ eyes, ________ nose, ________

teeth and ________ mouth.

____

____

____.

____

____

____.

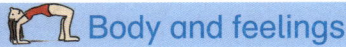

3. Draw your own planet and describe it.

____

____

4. Answer the questions.

How do you feel when you don't have breakfast?

I feel ______________________.

How do you feel when you get up very early?

I feel ______________________.

How do you feel when your favourite toy breaks?

______________________.

How do you feel when you lose your mum?

______________________.

How do you feel when your grandparents come to visit?

______________________.

Comic

Games at night

In the morning …

Tidy up your room, Jenny!

In the afternoon …

I put the racing cars under the bed, the cards on the desk and the skipping rope in the box.

At night …

PLING

PLING

Let's play cards!

Let's have a race!

Let's skip rope!

Wake up, Jenny!

Jennyyyyy!!! Tidy up your room!

?

1. Read and draw lines.

The dolls	are having a race.
The teddy bears	is angry.
The racing cars	are skipping rope.
The mother	sleeps at night.
Jenny	are playing cards.

ball **bike** **book** **castle** **computer game** **doll** **helicopter** **inline skates** **to play cards** **racing car** **skateboard** **to skip rope** **spaceship** **to swap stickers** **teddy bear** **toy**

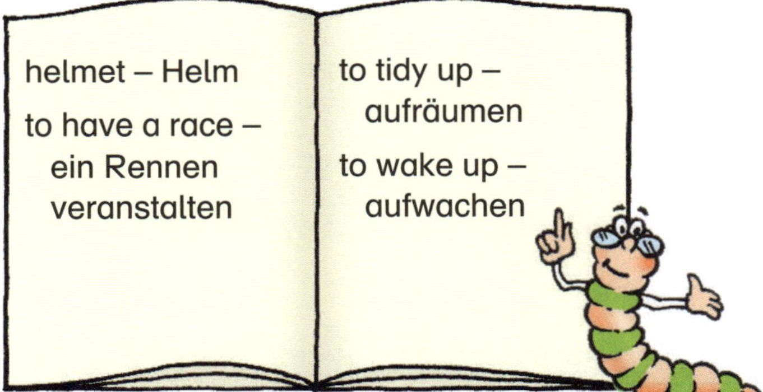
helmet – Helm
to have a race – ein Rennen veranstalten
to tidy up – aufräumen
to wake up – aufwachen

2. Jenny's room is tidy now. Where are the toys? Write.

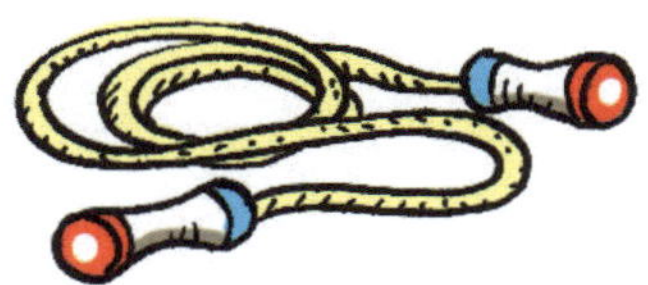

Wo sind die Spielsachen, nachdem Jenny ihr Zimmer aufgeräumt hat?

Bei Einzahl verwendest du *is*, bei Mehrzahl *are*.

The skipping rope is ______________________________.

The cars are ______________________________.

The cards ______________________________.

3. Which word is wrong? Cross it out.

I ~~doll~~ play football with my ball.
The teddy bear is blue my favourite toy.
I like swapping stickers five with my friends.
sing I don't like dolls.

 4. Which toy is it? Read, draw and write.

My favourite toy is blue, red and yellow.

You can play football or handball with it.

It's a ______________________.

My favourite toy is brown, soft and hairy.

It's a ______________________.

Löse die Rätsel und male das Spielzeug.

5. Look at the toys. Ask for the prices. Write.

How much is the ball? It's 30 p.

How much is the ____________________? It's 10 p.

____________________? It's £ 1.

____________________? It's 60 p.

____________________? It's 80 p.

____________________? It's 50 p.

6. Do the crossword.

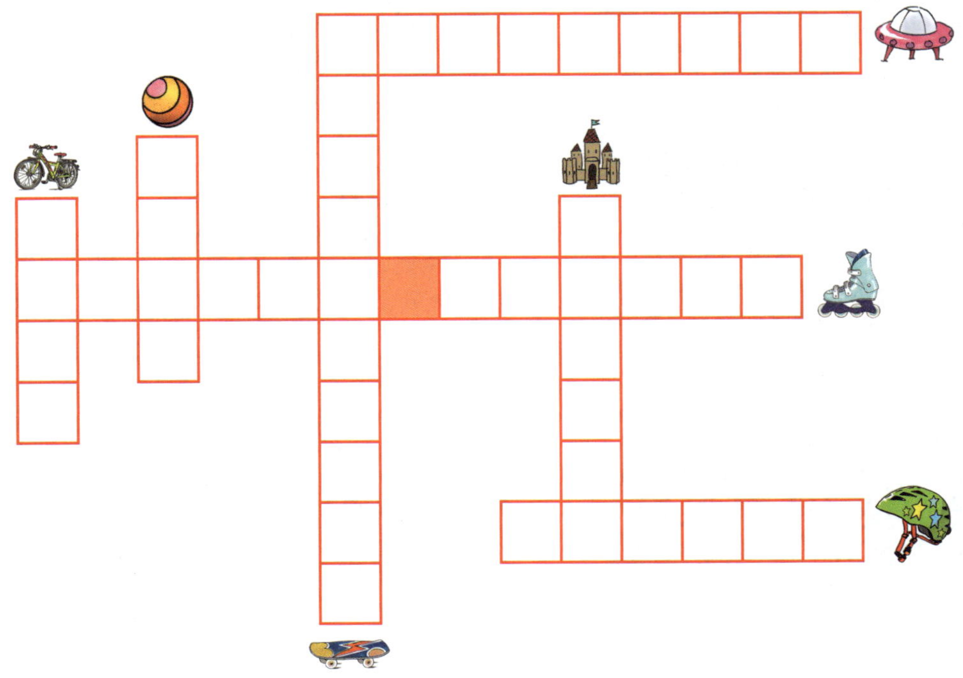

Comic

The designer contest

Hello everybody! Today we're looking for the super-designer.

Hi guys. I'm the best! Look at my golden and silver suit. Isn't it cool?

I don't like golden hats.
3
0
4

Here comes my outfit. I'm wearing green trousers and a green dress. Look at my sandals and my feathered headdress. I call it Green Bear.

I don't like green.
0
4
2

Hi, I'm Sally. I'm wearing my brown kangaroo jacket, my brown kangaroo trousers, my brown kanga-roo trainers and my lollipop sunglasses.

clap
hurray
10
clap
10
10

You are our new super-designer!

1. True or false? Tick ✓.

	true	false
In the jury there are a zebra, a giraffe and a crocodile.	○	○
The koala likes green.	○	○
Sally is the super-designer.	○	○
The jury likes the koala best.	○	○
The crocodile is wearing a red scarf and red shoes.	○	○
The giraffe doesn't like golden hats.	○	○
Sally is wearing ice-cream sunglasses.	○	○

boots cap coat dress gloves hat jacket (pair of) jeans pullover pyjamas scarf shirt shoes (pair of) shorts skirt socks T-shirt (pair of) trousers woolly hat to put on to take off to wear

colourful – bunt
feathered headdress – Federkopfschmuck
golden – gold
sandals – Sandalen
silver – silber
suit – Anzug
trainers – Turnschuhe

2. What's wrong? Circle the words.

Hi girls. I'm the best. Look at my yellow and red suit. Isn't it cold?

Here comes my dress. I'm wearing green shorts and a green skirt. Look at your sandals and your feathered headdress. I call it Green Grass.

3. It's winter . What's wrong? Anne changes her clothes.

to take off = ausziehen
to put on = anziehen

She puts on her ______________. She takes off her ______________.

She ______________

______________.

She ______________

______________.

She ______________

______________.

She ______________

______________.

She ______________

______________.

She ______________

____

______________.

Bei *he, she* oder *it* musst du an das Verb ein -s anhängen: *He puts on a jacket. She takes off her hat. It likes brown.*

 4. Look at Maggie, Jill and Sue. Read and find out who is who. What are they wearing? Colour.

__________ __________ __________

The girl with the green skirt is wearing a blue cap.
Jill doesn't like skirts.
The sandals are blue.
Jill doesn't like blue.
Sue's trainers are blue.
The other trainers are black.
Maggie's cap is yellow.
The woolly hat is green.
Sue is wearing a red T-shirt.
The other T-shirt is orange.
Maggie's trousers are blue, the other trousers are green.
The pullover is purple.

What is Maggie wearing? Write.

Maggie is wearing ______________________________

____.

Comic

A rainy birthday party

A hot and sunny day …

It's my birthday today. I'm so looking forward to my party. I want to have a party in the garden.

Where is the sun? Oh no, it's getting cloudy.

It's windy …

Sally, it's too windy for a party in the garden.

It's rainy …

Oh no! Hurry up. Let's go inside. It's starting to rain.

I hate rainy weather!

Sorry I'm late, but I've got the best present ever. Come in the garden with me.

The rain has stopped, it's sunny again.

What a wonderful rainbow! I love rainbows. Thank you so much for the beautiful birthday present.

1. Number the speech bubbles in the correct order.

Oh no! Hurry up. Let's go inside. It's starting to rain.
Where is the sun? Oh no, it's getting cloudy.
Sorry I'm late, but I've got the best present ever. Come in the garden with me.

☐ ☐ ☐

2. What's wrong? Cross out.

It's Sally's Halloween party / birthday party.

At the party it's raining / snowing.

At the end of the party it's sunny / foggy.

Sally loves rainy weather / rainbows.

Streiche jeweils die falsche Aussage durch.

rain rainbow snow sun cloudy foggy rainy snowy sunny windy cold hot to rain weather Monday Tuesday Wednesday Thursday Friday Saturday Sunday day weekend

beautiful – wunderschön
to hate – hassen
inside – drinnen
to look forward to – sich auf etwas freuen
rainbow – Regenbogen

I'm late. – Ich bin zu spät.
It's getting … – Es wird …
the best present ever – das allerbester Geschenk

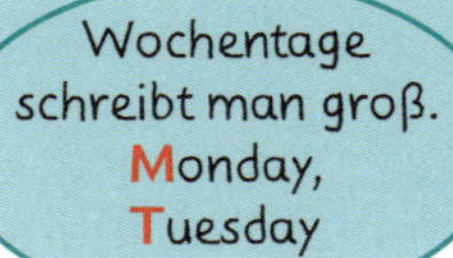
Wochentage
schreibt man groß.
Monday,
Tuesday

3. Read the words. Write.

M☺nd☺y ____________________

Wednesday ____________________

☺a☺u☺☺a☺ ____________________

Friday ____________________

T✱e✱d✱y ____________________

☼day ____________________

dayursTh ____________________

Monday ☼ 24°C
Tuesday 20°C
Wednesday 16°C
Thursday 15°C
Friday 18°C

4. Look and write.

On ____________ it's ____________.

On ____________ it's ____________ and ____________.

On ____________ it's ____________.

On ____________ it's ____________ and ____________.

On ____________ it's ____________ and ____________.

Liebe Kinder,

herzlichen Glückwunsch! Ihr habt nun schon so viel Englisch gelernt, dass ihr ganz alleine mit den Englisch-Stars für Profis arbeiten könnt.
In diesem Heft findet ihr 15 lustige, spannende und interessante Geschichten im Comicformat und zahlreiche Übungen und Rätsel rund um das Thema der Geschichten.

Was kannst du mit diesem Heft machen?

- Nimm dir dieses Heft im Unterricht immer dann, wenn du mit deinen Aufgaben schon fertig bist, oder zu Hause, wenn du noch mehr üben willst. Denn du weißt ja: Übung macht den Meister.
- Suche dir zunächst den Comic heraus, der am besten zu dem Thema passt, das ihr gerade im Unterricht behandelt. Also z. B. „Numbers" oder „At school". Ein kleines Zeichen (Icon) am oberen Ende der Seite zeigt dir das Thema an.
- Lies den Comic entweder zunächst alleine durch oder gemeinsam mit einem Partner. Die meisten Wörter in den Comics dürftest du kennen. Solltest du ein Wort mal nicht verstehen, dann versuche, es dir über die Bilder oder den Kontext zu erschließen. Wenn das nicht klappt, dann kannst du im „Wörterbuch" auf der nächsten Seite nachsehen. Dort findest du die Übersetzungen für unbekannte Wörter.
  Du kannst dir die Comics auch anhören. Bitte deine Eltern, dafür die Audio-Dateien aus dem Internet herunterzuladen.
- Anschließend bearbeitest du die nachfolgenden Seiten mit den Übungen. Fange hier am besten immer mit der ersten Übung an, denn in dieser kannst du feststellen, ob du den Comic richtig verstanden hast oder ob du ihn besser nochmal liest.
- Mit dem Lösungsheft kannst du nachsehen, ob du alle Aufgaben richtig gelöst hast.

Und zum Schluss möchte sich noch Willi, der schlaue Wurm, bei dir vorstellen. Er begleitet dich, neben Sally, dem Känguru, in diesem Heft und erinnert dich an wichtige Regeln im Englischen oder gibt dir Tipps.

Informationen für Eltern und Lehrkräfte:

Liebe Eltern, liebe Lehrkräfte,

die Englisch-Stars für Profis sind als differenzierendes Material für Schülerinnen und Schüler gedacht, die schon gut mit der englischen Sprache zurechtkommen und etwas mehr üben möchten. Da im Unterricht oft wenig Zeit zum selbstständigen Lesen bleibt, das Lesen aber ein wichtiger Bestandteil des Fremdsprachenlernens ist, sollen die Englisch-Stars für Profis diese Lücke schließen. Jedes Kapitel beginnt deshalb mit einem thematisch zum Unterricht passenden Comic. Diese sollen von den Kindern alleine oder gemeinsam mit einem Partner gelesen werden. Die meisten Wörter in den Comics sind bekannt. Unbekannte Wörter erschließen sich die Kinder aus dem Kontext. Ebenfalls wird eine Übersetzung neuer Wörter angeboten. Die Comics finden Sie auch als Audio-Dateien zum Herunterladen unter **www.cornelsen.de** unter dem Titel „Englisch-Stars Für Profis".
Weitere Aussprachehilfen bieten die gängigen digitalen Vokabeltrainer und Wörterbücher.
Fragen zum Text und weitere Übungen zur Festigung von Vokabeln, zum Leseverstehen, Schreiben und zum Sprechen folgen den Geschichten.
Nach dem Lesen und der Bearbeitung der Aufgaben können sich die Kinder Belohnungssterne ins Heft kleben.
Das integrierte Lösungsheft ermöglicht die Selbstkontrolle.
Willi, der Wurm, begleitet die Kinder und gibt wichtige Tipps und Hinweise.
Die Englisch-Stars für Profis sind die optimale Vorbereitung für die weiterführende Schule.

Lösungen

Comic

I like colours

What a grey day today. I don't like grey.
I've got an idea!
The sky is blue.
The sun is yellow.
The tree is green and brown.
The flowers are red, orange and pink.
What a colourful day. I like colours. And I like me.

1. True or false? Tick ✓.

	true	false
The sky is green.		✓
Sally likes grey.		✓
The sun is yellow.	✓	
The flowers are pink, red and orange.	✓	
Sally is black.		✓

Richtig oder falsch? Mache einen Haken.

2. Write.

What colour is the (sun)? The sun is yellow.

What colour is the (sky)? The sky is blue.

What colour is the (tree)? The tree is green and brown.

What colour are the (flowers)? The flowers are red, orange and pink.

What colour is Sally? Sally is yellow, blue, green, brown, red, orange and pink.

Schau dir nochmal den Comic an und schreibe die Farben der Dinge auf. Und Sally?

black blue brown
green grey orange
pink purple
red white yellow

colourful – bunt
day – Tag
flowers – Blumen
idea – Idee
sky – Himmel
sun – Sonne
tree – Baum

3. Read. Write in the correct colour.

green	green (grün)	black	black (schwarz)
red	red (rot)	grey	grey (grau)
blue	blue (blau)	purple	purple (lila)
pink	pink (rosa)	brown	brown (braun)
orange	orange (orange)	yellow	yellow (gelb)

Schreibe die Wörter in der richtigen Farbe.

4. Colour the picture. Write.

(individuelle Lösung)

The sky is __________.

The sun is __________.

The tree is __________.

The flowers are __________.

Sally is __________.

Which colour do you like best?

I ♥ __________ best.

Male das Bild an und vervollständige die Sätze.

Comic

The number code

SNIFF SNIFF
SCHOOL
Hey Tim, what's the matter?
I've got a new lock for my bike. But I don't remember the number code.
Try your birthday…
1, 5, 1, 2…No, that's not the correct number code.
Try the first four numbers of your telephone number.
3, 9, 8, 2… No, that's not the correct number code.
Try even numbers only.
2, 4, 6, 8…No, that's not the correct number code.
I'm such an idiot. I have absolutely no idea.
Zero,
zero,
zero idea…
CLICK
Yeah… That's it… Zero, zero, zero, zero!

1. True or false? Tick ✓.

	true	false
Tim has got a new bike.		✓
Tim doesn't remember his number code.	✓	
Tim's birthday is in December.	✓	
Tim's telephone number starts with 3.	✓	
The correct number code is 9999.		✓

2. Which tips do the children give Tim? Tick ✓.

Welche Ratschläge geben die Kinder Tim? Mache Haken.

Try…

- [x] your birthday.
- [x] the first four numbers of your telephone number.
- [ ] your mum's birthday.
- [ ] odd numbers.
- [x] even numbers.

123 one two three four five six seven eight nine ten eleven twelve

even numbers – gerade Zahlen
idea – Idee
lock – Schloss
number code – Zahlencode
odd numbers – ungerade Zahlen
to try – versuchen
zero – Null
That's it! – Das ist es!
What's the matter – Was ist los?

3. Read and write the numbers.

Alle geraden Zahlen (*even numbers*) kannst du durch zwei teilen. Ungerade Zahlen (*odd numbers*) nicht.

Write these numbers in the correct order:
seven, two, twelve, nine, ten, four, six, eight

two, four, six, seven, eight, nine, ten, twelve

Write down all even numbers from 1 – 12:

two four, six, eight, ten, twelve

Write down all odd numbers from 1 – 12:

one three, five, seven, nine, eleven

4. Colour.

(gelb) (rosa) (gelb) (rosa) (gelb) (grau) (rot) (grün) (weiß) (lila) (braun) (grau) (orange) (schwarz) (schwarz)

one	= blue
two	= green
three	= yellow
four	= pink
five	= brown
six	= grey
seven	= red
eight	= orange
nine	= purple
ten	= red
eleven	= black
twelve	= white

Comic

Where is the chalk?

Where is my chalk? Can you help me find it, please?
Little Red Riding Hood, have you got my chalk?
Sorry, no, I haven't. I've just got a book, a ruler, a glue stick, a cake and some flowers.
Frog Prince, have you got my chalk?
Sorry, no, I haven't. I've just got a pair of scissors, a rubber, a pen and a golden ball.
Cinderella, have you got my chalk?
Sorry, no, I haven't. I've just got a pencil case, a green pencil, a folder and a shoe.
Sleeping Beauty, have you got my chalk?
Sorry, no, I haven't. I've just got a red pencil, a ruler, a rubber and a spindle.
Sorry, I like to eat chalk.

1. What belongs together? Colour.

(blau) Der Wolf und die sieben Geißlein
(gelb) [spindle]
(rot) [basket]
(gelb) Dornröschen
(grün) [well]
Aschenputtel (orange)
Cinderella (orange)
The Frog Prince (grün)
(rot) Little Red Riding Hood
(gelb) Sleeping Beauty
(rot) Rotkäppchen
(orange) [shoe]
[wolf and kids] (blau)
(blau) The wolf and the seven young kids
Froschkönig (grün)

Male die drei Kästen, die jeweils zusammengehören in derselben Farbe aus.

board book chair chalk computer desk folder glue stick pen pencil pencil case pencil sharpener rubber ruler scissors schoolbag pupil school uniform teacher art maths music science sports subject

cake – Kuchen
flowers – Blumen
golden ball – goldene Kugel
shoe – Schuh
spindle – Spindel

Schau dir den Comic nochmal an und schreibe auf, welche Schulsachen die Märchenfiguren jeweils haben.

2. What school things have they got? Write.

Little Red Riding Hood has got a ruler, a book and a glue stick.

Cinderella has got a pencil case, a green pencil and a folder.

The Frog Prince has got a pair of scissors, a rubber and a pen.

Sleeping Beauty has got a red pencil, a ruler and a rubber.

3. Read and colour the school things.

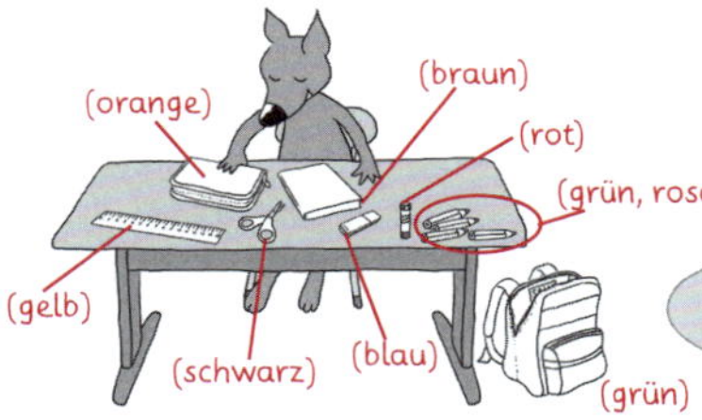

(orange) (braun) (rot) (grün, rosa, schwarz, lila) (gelb) (schwarz) (blau) (grün)

Lies und male die Schulsachen in den richtigen Farben aus.

My schoolbag is green and my pencil case is orange.
My scissors are black and my rubber is blue.
My glue stick is red.
My book is brown and the ruler is yellow.
My pencils are green, pink, black and purple.

4. Look and write.

The book is **under** the basket.

The ruler is **on** the basket.

The pencil case is **in** the basket.

Lies den Text und setze die Wörter ein.

5. Read and fill in the gaps.

ends sports friends morning

Hello, my name is Nick. I go to Westminster school.
I'm in class 3c. My teacher is Mrs Green. My school uniform
is blue and white. School starts at 9 o'clock in the morning
and ends at 4 o'clock in the afternoon. Every morning we have
assembly. At 12.30 it's lunchtime. I eat at school with my friends.
I like sports and music best.

teacher uniform name starts school class

Now it's your turn. Fill in.

Hello, my name is (Name). I go to (Schule) school.
I'm in class (Klasse). My teacher is Mr. / Mrs. (Lehrkraft).
School starts at (Uhrzeit) and ends at (Uhrzeit).
I like (Lieblingsfach).

(individuelle Lösung)

Comic

Let's be happy!

At night Tommy doesn't sleep in his bed ...
... He flies into space in his pot and looks for new planets.
Hello, I'm Tommy. Are you all right?
I'm so sad. I'm so lonely. I haven't got any friends.
PLASH
Go away! I'm angry! Nobody likes me. I haven't got any friends.
GRRRR
Why are you so tired?
It's so boring. I haven't got any friends.
ZZZ
I've got an idea!
PLEASE COME TO MY PLANET PARTY
We are all happy now. We are all friends.

1. True or false? Tick ✓.

	true	false
At night Tommy sleeps in his pot.		✓
Tommy is flying in his pot.	✓	
The green planet is angry.		✓
The red planet is angry.	✓	
The blue planet is tired.		✓
All the planets are sad in the end.		✓
The planets are having a birthday party.		✓

Die Mehrzahl von Nomen bildet man, in dem man ein -s an das Wort hängt z.B. 1 arm – 2 arms, 1 leg – 2 legs
Es gibt aber auch unregelmäßige Nomen z.B. 1 foot – 2 feet, 1 tooth – 2 teeth

arm ear eye
foot – feet hand
leg mouth nose
tooth – teeth
angry happy
hungry sad
scared tired

boring – langweilig
to fly – fliegen
idea – Idee
lonely – einsam
night – Nacht
pot – Topf
to sleep – schlafen
space – Weltall
planet – Planet
Go away! – Geh weg!

2. Describe the planets. Write.

Schau dir die Planeten genau an und beschreibe sie.

The red planet has got six hands, two eyes, one nose, three teeth and one mouth.

The blue planet has got two hands, two eyes, one nose, one mouth and four legs.

The white planet has got two hands, two eyes, one nose and three mouths.

3. Draw your own planet and describe it.

(individuelle Lösung)

4. Answer the questions.

How do you feel when you don't have breakfast?
I feel hungry.

Milk

How do you feel when you get up very early?
I feel tired.

05:00

How do you feel when your favourite toy breaks?
I feel sad.

How do you feel when you lose your mum?
I feel scared.

How do you feel when your grandparents come to visit?
I feel happy.

Comic

Games at night

Tidy up your room, Jenny!

In the morning …

In the afternoon …

I put the racing cars under the bed, the cards on the desk and the skipping rope in the box.

At night …

PLING

PLING

Let's play cards!

Let's have a race!

Let's skip rope!

Wake up, Jenny!

Jennyyyyy!!! Tidy up your room!

?

1. Read and draw lines.

The dolls	are having a race.
The teddy bears	is angry.
The racing cars	are skipping rope.
The mother	sleeps at night.
Jenny	are playing cards.

ball bike book castle computer game doll helicopter inline skates to play cards racing car skateboard to skip rope spaceship to swap stickers teddy bear toy

helmet – Helm
to have a race – ein Rennen veranstalten
to tidy up – aufräumen
to wake up – aufwachen

2. Jenny's room is tidy now. Where are the toys? Write.

Wo sind die Spielsachen nachdem Jenny ihr Zimmer aufgeräumt hat?

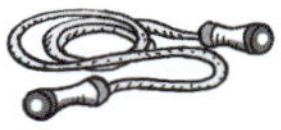

Bei Einzahl verwendest du is, bei Mehrzahl are.

The skipping rope is in the box.

The cars are under the bed.

The cards are on the desk.

Lösungen

3. Which word is wrong? Cross it out.

I ~~doll~~ play football with my ball.
The teddy bear is ~~blue~~ my favourite toy.
I like swapping stickers ~~five~~ with my friends.
~~sing~~ I don't like dolls.

4. Which toy is it? Read, draw and write.

My favourite toy is blue, red and yellow.

You can play football or handball with it.

(Ball)

It's a ball.

My favourite toy is brown, soft and hairy.

(Teddybär)

It's a teddy bear.

Löse die Rätsel und male das Spielzeug.

5. Look at the toys. Ask for the prices. Write.

30 p
80 p
10 p
£ 1
60 p
50 p

How much is the ball?	It's 30 p.
How much is the book?	It's 10 p.
How much is the helicopter?	It's £ 1.
How much is the car?	It's 60 p.
How much is the doll?	It's 80 p.
How much is the teddy bear?	It's 50 p.

6. Do the crossword.

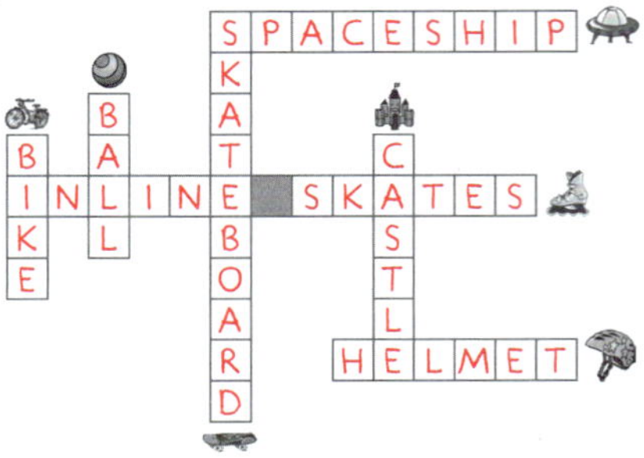

SPACESHIP
SKATEBOARD
BALL
BIKE
INLINE SKATES
CASTLE
HELMET

Comic

The designer contest

Hello everybody! Today we're looking for the super-designer.
Hi guys. I'm the best! Look at my golden and silver suit. Isn't it cool?
I don't like golden hats.
Here comes my outfit. I'm wearing green trousers and a green dress. Look at my sandals and my feathered headdress. I call it Green Bear.
I don't like green.
Hi, I'm Sally. I'm wearing my brown kangaroo jacket, my brown kangaroo trousers, my brown kangaroo trainers and my lollipop sunglasses.
clap hurray clap
You are our new super-designer!

1. True or false? Tick ✓.

	true	false
In the jury there are a zebra, a giraffe and a crocodile.		✓
The koala likes green.	✓	
Sally is the super-designer.	✓	
The jury likes the koala best.		✓
The crocodile is wearing a red scarf and red shoes.	✓	
The giraffe doesn't like golden hats.	✓	
Sally is wearing ice-cream sunglasses.		✓

boots cap coat dress gloves hat jacket (pair of) jeans pullover pyjamas scarf shirt shoes (pair of) shorts skirt socks T-shirt (pair of) trousers woolly hat to put on to take off to wear

colourful – bunt
feathered headdress – Federkopfschmuck
golden – gold
sandals – Sandalen
silver – silber
suit – Anzug
trainers – Turnschuhe

2. What's wrong? Circle the words.

Hi girls. I'm the best. Look at my yellow and red suit. Isn't it cold?

Here comes my dress. I'm wearing green shorts and a green skirt. Look at your sandals and your feathered headdress. I call it Green Grass.

3. It's winter. What's wrong? Anne changes her clothes.

to take off = ausziehen
to put on = anziehen

She puts on her pullover. She takes off her T-shirt.

She puts on her trousers. She takes off her skirt.

She puts on her boots. She takes off her sandals/shoes.

She puts on her jacket.

She puts on her woolly hat.

Bei *he*, *she* oder *it* musst du an das Verb ein -s anhängen: *He puts on a jacket. She takes off her hat. It likes brown.*

4. Look at Maggie, Jill and Sue. Read and find out who is who. What are they wearing? Colour.

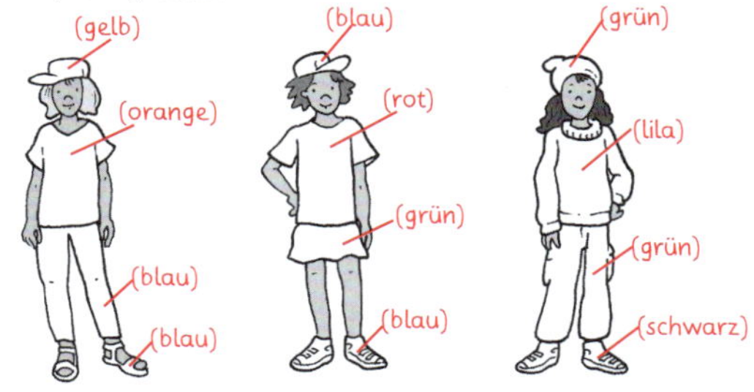

(gelb) (orange) (blau) (blau) — Maggie

(blau) (rot) (grün) (blau) — Sue

(grün) (lila) (grün) (schwarz) — Jill

The girl with the green skirt is wearing a blue cap.
Jill doesn't like skirts.
The sandals are blue.
Jill doesn't like blue.
Sue's trainers are blue.
The other trainers are black.
Maggie's cap is yellow.
The woolly hat is green.
Sue is wearing a red T-shirt.
The other T-shirt is orange.
Maggie's trousers are blue, the other trousers are green.
The pullover is purple.

What is Maggie wearing? Write.

Maggie is wearing a yellow cap, an orange T-Shirt, blue trousers and blue sandals.

Comic

A rainy birthday party

A hot and sunny day ...
It's my birthday today. I'm so looking forward to my party. I want to have a party in the garden.
Where is the sun? Oh no, it's getting cloudy.
It's windy ...
Sally, it's too windy for a party in the garden.
It's rainy ...
Oh no! Hurry up. Let's go inside. It's starting to rain.
I hate rainy weather!
Sorry I'm late, but I've got the best present ever. Come in the garden with me.
The rain has stopped, it's sunny again.
What a wonderful rainbow! I love rainbows. Thank you so much for the beautiful birthday present.

1. Number the speech bubbles in the correct order.

Oh no! Hurry up. Let's go inside. It's starting to rain. — 2

Where is the sun? Oh no, it's getting cloudy. — 1

Sorry I'm late, but I've got the best present ever. Come in the garden with me. — 3

2. What's wrong? Cross out.

It's Sally's ~~Halloween party~~ / birthday party.

At the party it's raining / ~~snowing~~.

At the end of the party it's sunny / ~~foggy~~.

Sally loves ~~rainy weather~~ / rainbows.

Streiche jeweils die falsche Aussage durch.

rain rainbow snow sun cloudy foggy rainy snowy sunny windy cold hot to rain weather Monday Tuesday Wednesday Thursday Friday Saturday Sunday day weekend

beautiful – wunderschön
to hate – hassen
inside – drinnen
to look forward to – sich auf etwas freuen
rainbow – Regenbogen
I'm late. – Ich bin zu spät.
It's getting ... – Es wird ...
the best present ever – das allerbester Geschenk

Wochentage schreibt man groß. Monday, Tuesday

3. Read the words. Write.

M☺nd☺y Monday

Wednesday Wednesday

☺a☺u☺☺a☺ Saturday

Friday Friday

T✱e✱d✱y Tuesday

☀day Sunday

dayursTh Thursday

4. Look and write.

Monday 24°C
Tuesday 20°C
Wednesday 16°C
Thursday 15°C
Friday 18°C

On Monday it's sunny.

On Tuesday it's sunny and cloudy.

On Wednesday it's rainy.

On Thursday it's rainy and windy.

On Friday it's sunny and windy.

5. Read the sentences. Write a family plan.

On Monday I do yoga.

On Saturday I play tennis.

On Wednesday I play with my band.

I go inline skating on Tuesday.

On Friday I go swimming.

I go to the doctor on Thursday.

On Sunday I go to the museum with Emma, Kate and Ben.

Mon	Tue	Wed	Thu	Fri	Sat	Sun
Mum - yoga!	Emma – inline skating	Ben – band	Mum – doctor	Kate – swimming	Dad – tennis	Dad, Emma, Kate, Ben – museum

My Calendar

Comic

The new baby

Hi, I'm Rocky.

These are my mum and my dad and my newborn baby sister Milly.

Today everybody is coming to see Milly. Uncle Mac and Aunt Emma are coming.

What a cute baby!

Here is a present for Milly. It's a bow and arrow!

Grandpa Woody and Grandma Wally are coming, too.

Hello everybody! Here is a present for Milly. It's an egg.

Cousin Stoney is coming to the party, too.

Hi! What a lovely baby! Here is a present for Milly. It's a dinosaur. Be careful...

CRACK!

...this little dinosaur can spit fire...

1. Who brings which present? Colour.

Wer bringt welches Geschenk? Male die beiden Kästen die jeweils zusammengehören in derselben Farbe aus.

bow and arrow (rot) – Uncle Mac and Aunt Emma

egg (blau) – Grandpa Woody and Grandma Wally

dinosaur (gelb) – Cousin Stoney

2. Read and correct the sentences.

Was stimmt nicht? Schreibe die Sätze richtig auf.

Milly is a dinosaur.

Milly is a baby.

Uncle Mac and Sister Emma are coming.

Uncle Mac and Aunt Emma are coming.

Rocky gets presents.

Milly gets presents.

The dinosaur can't spit fire.

The dinosaur can spit fire.

family friend boy girl brother sister mother/mum father/dad grandfather/grandpa grandmother/grandma aunt uncle cousin

arrow – Pfeil
bow – Bogen
to be careful – vorsichtig sein
cave – Höhle
egg – Ei
present – Geschenk
to spit fire – Feuer spucken
surprise – Überraschung

3. Who is it? Write.

She is my mum's mother. She is my grandmother/grandma.
Her name is Wally.

He is my mum's father. He is my grandfather/grandpa.
His name is Woody.

Can you guess who it is?

Her name is Milly. She is my sister.

He is my dad's brother. He is my uncle.
His name is Mac.

She is the daughter of my dad's brother. She is my cousin.
Her name is Stoney.

4. Read the words. Write.

br th r	mother
brother	mother
cousin	a n
cousin	aunt
a	fatherandgr
dad	grandfather

5. Describe your family.

I've got a mother, a father and a sister. What about you?

I've got (individuelle Lösung).

6. Read and write.

My best friend is green. He has got 2 legs and can spit fire.

My best friend's name is Tom. He is a boy. He has got brown hair and brown eyes. He is wearing a green T-shirt and blue jeans. I like him, because he's funny.

My best friend is a girl. She has got long black hair and dark eyes. She is from Japan. I like her because she is clever.

My best friend is a girl. She has got short blond hair and green eyes. She loves to wear dresses and to read books. I like her because we play tennis together.

dresses boy brown Japan eyes (2x) jeans green legs name like hair best has got T-shirt clever books tennis girl fire

Comic

What a morning!

It's early Sunday morning.

Sally opens the fridge.

Oh no! No milk for hot chocolate. No orange juice, no ham, no eggs, no jam.

No cornflakes, no honey, no bread, no breakfast.

Sally is sad.

It's not my day today. I'm going back to bed.

Here comes Koala.

Breakfast for Sally.

Oh Koala, I like hot chocolate and eggs, toast with jam and orange juice for breakfast. But I like you best!

1. What does Koala bring for breakfast. Read and tick ✓.

For breakfast Koala brings …

☐ hot chocolate, eggs, toast with honey, orange juice

☐ hot chocolate, eggs, toast with jam, apple juice

✓ hot chocolate, eggs, toast with jam, orange juice

Finde das richtige Tablett und kreuze es an.

2. What do you like for breakfast? Draw and write.

(individuelle Lösung)

bread breakfast butter cheese cornflakes egg ham honey jam roll toast drinks apple juice coffee coke hot chocolate lemonade milk orange juice tea water to eat to drink

3. Find the words. Write and draw lines.

orange juice
honey
coffee
bread
hot chocolate
egg

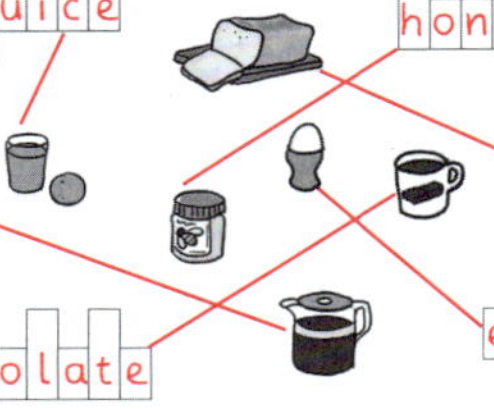

4. Read and colour. Find the matching answer for each question.

What do you have for breakfast? (blau)
Do you like milk in your tea? (rot)
Can I have the butter, please? (grün)
Would you like some cheese? (gelb)
Pass me the bacon, please. (orange)

Here you are. (orange)
For breakfast I have toast with ham. (blau)
Yes, please. (gelb)
No, I don't. I like sugar. (rot)
Here you are. (grün)

Male die Frage und die passende Antwort in derselben Farbe aus.

5. What do they say? Write the dialogue.

Wenn du Hilfe brauchst, schaue in Aufgabe 4 nach.

Betty
Jack

Frage Betty was sie zum Frühstück isst.
What do you have for breakfast?

Sage, dass du zum Frühstück Toast mit Käse isst.
For breakfast I have toast with cheese.

Frage Jack ob er Milch in seinem Tee mag.
Do you like milk in your tea?

Verneine.
No, I don't.

Bitte Jack dir den Honig zu reichen.
Can I have the honey, please?

Reiche Betty den Honig.
Here you are.

Comic

The fruit expert

Do melons grow on trees?
No, melons grow on the ground.
Why are bananas curved?
Because they grow towards the sun.
Do pineapples grow on apple trees?
No, they grow on the ground, like melons.
Now I'd like to have a fruit salad.
Me too. But where do we get the fruit from?
We've already got a watermelon, a banana and a pineapple. And in my pouch I've got apples, pears, strawberries, plums, ...

1. Read and circle the correct word.

Kreise das passende Wort ein, um den Satz zu vervollständigen.

Bananas are (curved) / round.
Melons grow on trees / (the ground).
Sally has got (fruit) / lollipops in her pouch.
Pineapples grow on trees / (the ground).

2. Write the name of the trees.

apple tree
plum tree
cherry tree

fruit apple banana cherry lemon melon
orange pear pineapple plum strawberry

ground – Boden
sun – Sonne
tree – Baum
curved – gebogen
to grow – wachsen
sour – sauer
sweet – süß

Fruit

2. Find the 10 fruit words. Circle and write.

s	t	r	a	w	b	e	r	r	y	l
r	p	i	n	e	a	p	p	l	e	p
o	k	a	d	g	h	o	t	b	p	z
r	p	p	e	a	r	w	r	y	h	l
a	o	f	b	a	n	a	n	a	j	e
n	u	s	e	i	u	w	s	p	m	m
g	k	b	g	a	c	o	b	p	o	o
e	y	p	l	u	m	l	k	l	y	n
t	c	a	h	y	w	e	a	e	d	a
c	h	e	r	r	y	y	l	s	a	b
t	i	p	d	n	z	m	e	l	o	n

strawberry, pineapple, orange, pear, banana,
apple, lemon, plum, cherry, melon

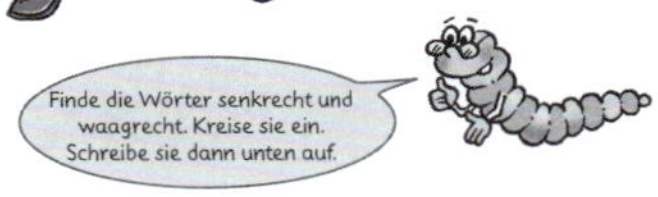

Finde die Wörter senkrecht und waagrecht. Kreise sie ein. Schreibe sie dann unten auf.

Fruit

3. Fill in.

Apples are red, green or yellow. They grow on trees.
Cherries are sour or sweet. Plums are purple and have got a stone inside. Bananas are curved because they grow towards the sun. Strawberries are red. They grow on the ground.
Melons grow on the ground, too. They are round and big.
Lemons grow on trees. They are sour.

purple green sun melons trees sweet ground sour

4. Read and write.

Which fruit grow on trees? (Beispiele)

apples, pears, plums, cherries

Which fruit grow on the ground?

melons, pineapples, strawberries

Which fruit are sweet?

cherries, apples, bananas, plums

Which fruit are sour?

lemons, cherries, apples

Which fruit do you like best?

(individuelle Lösung)

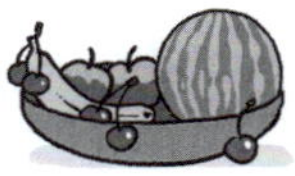

Pets

Comic

New friends

In the kitchen...
Mummy, what can I do? It's so boring!
Go out and play with your friends, Tom. But be back for dinner.
But nobody has time to play with Tom.
In the street...
Hey, little cat, do you want to be my new friend?
Miaow!
At the playground...
Hello!
Oh, a parrot! Do you want to be my new friend, too?
In the forest...
Hi tortoise. Do you want to be my new friend, too?
A dog! Do you want to be my new friend, too?
Bow, wow!
In front of Tom's house ...
I'm back with my friends. Can they have dinner with us?
Yes, sit down.
Oh, no!

Pets

1. Read and answer.

Schau dir nochmal den Comic an und beantworte die Fragen.

Where does Tom find the dog?

Toms finds the dog in front of the house.

What animal does Tom find at the playground?

Tom finds a parrot at the playground.

What colour is the parrot?

The parrot is red, yellow and green.

How many new friends has Tom got?

Tom has got five new friends.

Who are Tom's new friends?

Tom's new friends are a cat, a parrot, a tortoise and a dog.

pet budgie cat dog fish guinea pig hamster mouse rabbit tortoise ears legs big small fast slow long short brown black grey white

boring – langweilig
dinner – Abendessen
to fly – fliegen
forest – Wald
in front of – vor
kitchen – Küche
to meet – treffen
new – neu
playground – Spielplatz
street – Straße
to swim – schwimmen
time – Zeit
tail – Schwanz
wing – Flügel

2. Find my pet. Read and circle.

My cat is black and white with green eyes.

My dog is brown and big. It has got short ears.

My parrot is green and yellow. It likes to eat nuts.

My guinea pig is brown and white. It has got long hair.

3. Find the plural. Write.

one dog – two dogs

one fish – three fish

one hamster – two hamsters

one mouse – three mice

one guinea pig – four guinea pigs

one budgie – ten budgies

one cat – two cats

Die Mehrzahl von Nomen bildet man, indem man ein -s an das Wort hängt z. B. 1 dog – 2 dogs. Es gibt aber auch unregelmäßige Nomen: 1 fish – 3 fish; 1 mouse – 2 mice

4. Write 5 sentences.

Dogs		water.
Fish		milk.
Hamsters	drink	fly.
Budgies	can	swim.
Cats		

Dogs drink water / can swim.
Fish can swim.
Hamsters drink water.
Budgies drink water / can fly.
Cats drink water / milk.

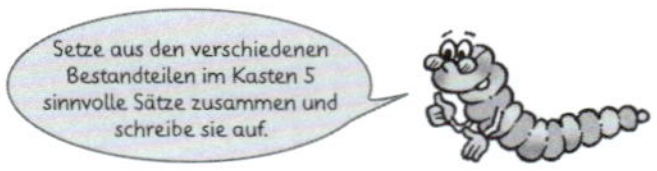

Setze aus den verschiedenen Bestandteilen im Kasten 5 sinnvolle Sätze zusammen und schreibe sie auf.

Comic

Sally, you are special, too!

Sally is on the farm.
I can't give milk.
Hello, I'm Tilda the cow. I can give milk. What about you?
I can't give wool.
Hello, I'm Sheila the sheep. I can give wool. What about you?
I can't lay eggs.
Hello, I'm Henny the hen. I can lay eggs. What about you?
Sally is sad.
Sally, what's the matter?
I'm sad. I can't give milk, I can't give wool and I can't lay eggs. I can't do anything special.
Miaow!
Oh no. We have to help the little cat.
Thank you Sally.
Sally, maybe you can't give milk, give wool or lay eggs. But you can jump up very high. You are special, too.

1. What can the animals do? Write sentences.

can

give wool.
give milk.
jump high.
lay eggs.

The hen can lay eggs.
The sheep can give wool.
Sally can jump high.
The cow can give milk.

cat cow dog duck goose – geese hen
horse pig sheep – sheep

to help – helfen
to give – geben
high – hoch
to lay eggs – Eier legen
wool – Wolle

2. Where do the words end? Circle and write.

horsecowpigdoggooseduckmousesheephen

horse, cow, pig, dog, goose, duck, mouse, sheep, hen

3. Which animal is it? Write.

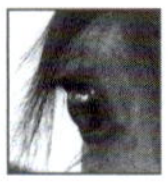

horse

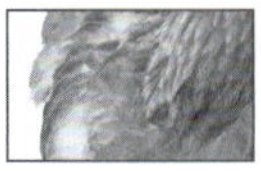

hen

pig

sheep

cow

4. Read and fill in.

A day on the farm

Farmer Jonny gets up at 5 o'clock in the morning. He milks the cows. He collects the eggs from the hens. He feeds the pigs and the geese. Then farmer Jonny brings the cows and the sheep outside so that they can eat the green grass. He makes butter from the milk. For his new warm pullover he takes the wool from the sheep. After a long day farmer Jonny is hungry. He drinks a glass of milk and he eats bread with ham and eggs. Now Jonny is tired and goes to bed.

geese pigs morning cows bed grass hens sheep drinks milk wool eats

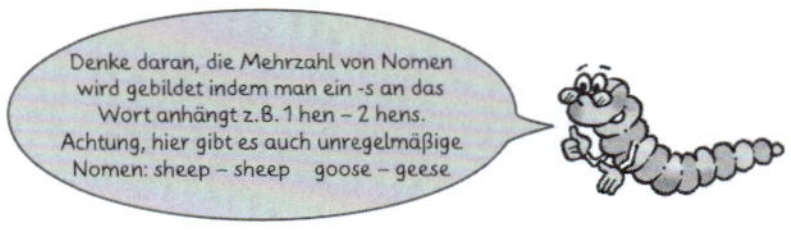

Denke daran, die Mehrzahl von Nomen wird gebildet indem man ein -s an das Wort anhängt z.B. 1 hen – 2 hens. Achtung, hier gibt es auch unregelmäßige Nomen: sheep – sheep goose – geese

Comic

Dangerous jelly fish

One day, the Millers are having a picnic on the beach.

What a nice day.

In the afternoon the Millers go home. But look at the beach: there is plastic everywhere

Oh no, what a mess!

Here comes a big wave.

Now all the plastic waste is in the sea.

What a yummy little fish.

I'm hungry. I'm going to eat this jelly fish.

Let me help you!

LIFE GUARD

Thank you for saving me!

Don't leave your plastic waste on the beach. Plastic kills our nature!

1. True or false? Tick ✓.

	true	false
The Millers are having a picnic on the beach.	✓	
Plastic bottles and plastic bags are in the sea.	✓	
The fish eats the plastic bag.		✓
The turtle helps the man.		✓
The man helps the turtle.	✓	
Plastic is good for our nature.		✓

beach fish nature picnic

bag – Tüte
bottle – Flasche
dangerous – gefährlich
to help – helfen
hungry – hungrig
jelly fish – Qualle
to kill – umbringen
to leave – zurücklassen
life guard – Rettungsschwimmer
plastic – Plastik
to save – retten
sea – Meer
turtle – Wasserschildkröte
waste – Abfall
wave – Welle
What a mess! – Was für eine Unordnung!
Yummy! – Lecker

Lösungen

2. What do they say? Look and write.

Oh no, what a mess!

Let me help you!

Thank you for saving me!

Schaue dir den Comic nochmal an und fülle die Sprechblasen aus.

3. What belongs into the sea? Circle.

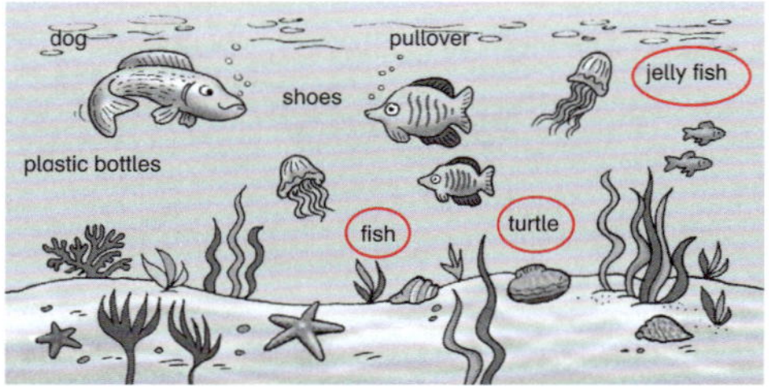

dog, pullover, shoes, jelly fish (circled), plastic bottles, fish (circled), turtle (circled)

Was gehört ins Meer? Kreise die passenden Wörter ein.

4. Do the crossword.

BAG, BOTTLE, LIFEGUARD, BEACH, TURTLE, JELLYFISH, FISH, SEA

5. Odd one out. Cross out the word that doesn't match.

~~cow~~	beach	bottle
fish	water	bag
turtle	~~garden~~	waste
jelly fish	wave	~~flower~~

Comic

The story of St. George

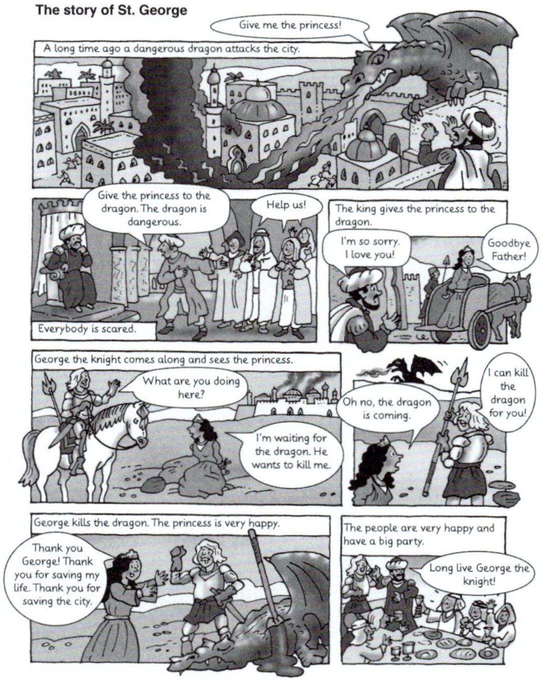

A long time ago a dangerous dragon attacks the city.

Give me the princess!

Give the princess to the dragon. The dragon is dangerous.

Help us!

Everybody is scared.

The king gives the princess to the dragon.

I'm so sorry. I love you!

Goodbye Father!

George the knight comes along and sees the princess.

What are you doing here?

I'm waiting for the dragon. He wants to kill me.

Oh no, the dragon is coming.

I can kill the dragon for you!

George kills the dragon. The princess is very happy.

Thank you George! Thank you for saving my life. Thank you for saving the city.

The people are very happy and have a big party.

Long live George the knight!

1. Read the comic. Fill in the gaps.

A dangerous dragon attacks the city. The king gives the princess to the dragon. George the knight sees the princess. The dragon wants to kill the princess. George fights against the dragon. He kills the dragon. The princess and the king are very happy. They have a big party in the city.

princess dragon (2x) king party kill George happy

Der heilige Georg ist der Schutzpatron von England. Im Union Jack kannst du das rote Georgskreuz erkennen.

Big Ben
Buckingham Palace
double-decker-bus
guard
London Eye
taxi
River Thamse
Tower Bridge
Tower of London
Union Jack

to attack – angreifen
city – Stadt
dangerous – gefährlich
dragon – Drache
to fight – kämpfen
to help – helfen
to kill – töten
knight – Ritter
life – Leben
map – Karte
people – Volk
to save – retten
sight – Sehenswürdikgkeiten

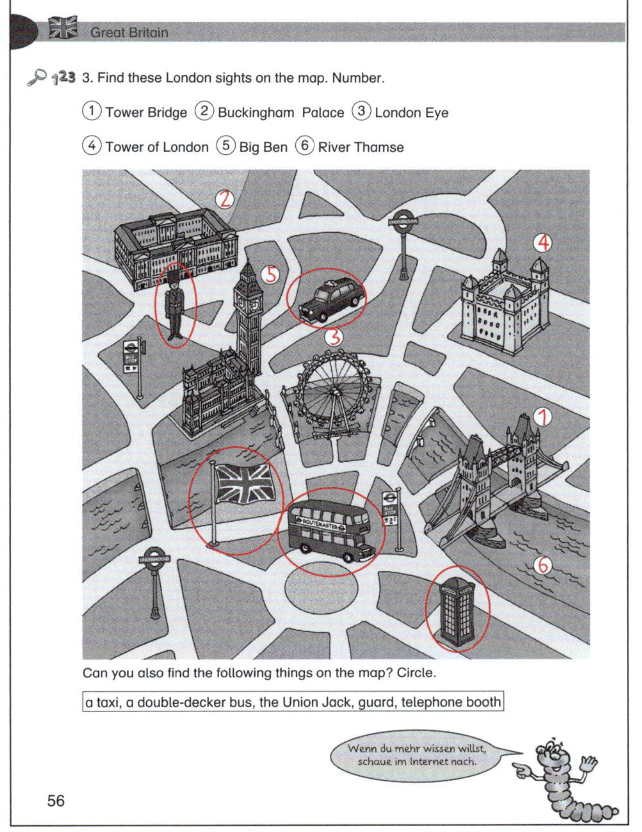

Great Britain
3. Find these London sights on the map. Number.
① Tower Bridge ② Buckingham Palace ③ London Eye
④ Tower of London ⑤ Big Ben ⑥ River Thamse
Can you also find the following things on the map? Circle.
a taxi, a double-decker bus, the Union Jack, guard, telephone booth
Wenn du mehr wissen willst, schaue im Internet nach.
56

Die Lösung zur Seite 3:

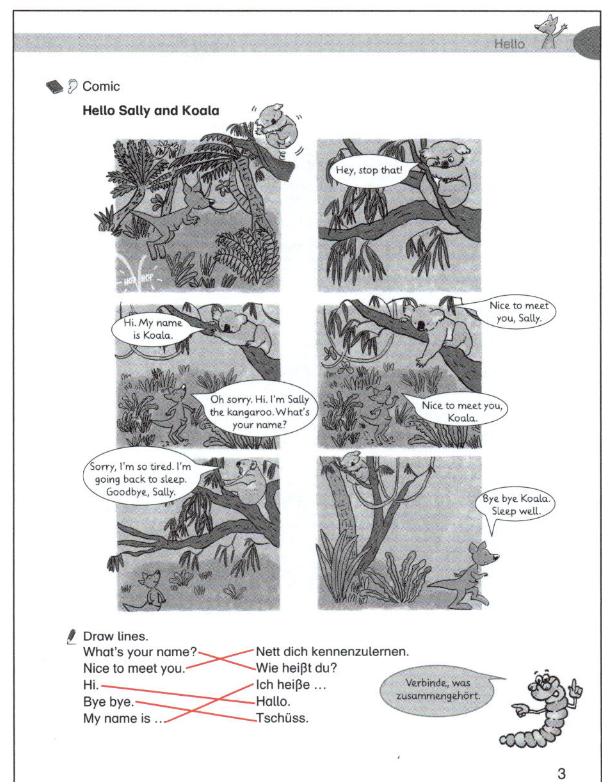

Hello
Comic
Hello Sally and Koala
Hey, stop that!
Hi. My name is Koala.
Oh sorry. Hi. I'm Sally the kangaroo. What's your name?
Nice to meet you, Sally.
Nice to meet you, Koala.
Sorry, I'm so tired. I'm going back to sleep. Goodbye, Sally.
Bye bye Koala. Sleep well.
Draw lines.
What's your name?
Nice to meet you.
Hi.
Bye bye.
My name is …
Nett dich kennenzulernen.
Wie heißt du?
Ich heiße …
Hallo.
Tschüss.
Verbinde, was zusammengehört.
3

Hast du Sally gefunden? Sie hat sich auf Seite 23 und auf Seite 45 versteckt.

Illustrationen:
Barbara Jung: S.3, S.4, S.6, S.12 (unten), S.21 (Raumschiff, Burg), S.22, S.24 (oben), S.26, S.34, S.36, S.38, S.40 (unten), S.41, S.46, S.47

Thilo Pustlauk: S.7, S.9, S.10, S.11, S.12 (oben), S.13, S.14, S.16, S.17, S.18, S.19, S.20, S.21 (alles bis auf Burg und Raumschiff), S.24 (unten), S.25, S.28, S.29, S.30, S.32, S.33, S.35, S.37, S.39, S.42, S.44, S.48, S.49 (Blume, Bauer beim Melken), S.50, S.52, S.53, S.54, S.55, S.56

Wilfried Poll: S.40 (oben), S.49 (Schwein, Gans, Schaf, Bett)

Wurm: Thilo Pustlauk

Kapitelvignetten: Wilfried Poll

Icons Wörterkästen: Thilo Pustlauk

Icons Aufgabenanweisungen: Wilfried Poll, Barbara Jung (Buch, Lupe)

5. Read the sentences. Write a family plan.

On Monday I do yoga.

On Saturday I play tennis.

On Wednesday I play with my band.

I go inline skating on Tuesday.

On Friday I go swimming.

I go to the doctor on Thursday.

On Sunday I go to the museum with Emma, Kate and Ben.

Mon	Tue	Wed	Thu	Fri	Sat	Sun
Mum-yoga!						

My Calendar

 Comic

The new baby

Hi, I'm Rocky.
These are my mum and my dad and my newborn baby sister Milly.

Today everybody is coming to see Milly. Uncle Mac and Aunt Emma are coming.

Grandpa Woody and Grandma Wally are coming, too.

Hello everybody! Here is a present for Milly. It's an egg.

Cousin Stoney is coming to the party, too.

Hi! What a lovely baby! Here is a present for Milly. It's a dinosaur. Be careful...

CRACK!

...this little dinosaur can spit fire...

1. Who brings which present? Colour.

Wer bringt welches Geschenk? Male die beiden Kästen, die jeweils zusammengehören, in derselben Farbe aus.

egg

dinosaur

bow and arrow

Uncle Mac and Aunt Emma

Grandpa Woody and Grandma Wally

Cousin Stoney

2. Read and correct the sentences.

Was stimmt nicht? Schreibe die Sätze richtig auf.

Milly is a dinosaur.

____

Uncle Mac and Sister Emma are coming.

____

Rocky gets presents.

____

The dinosaur can't spit fire.

____

family friend boy
girl brother sister
mother/mum
father/dad
grandfather/grandpa
grandmother/grandma
aunt uncle cousin

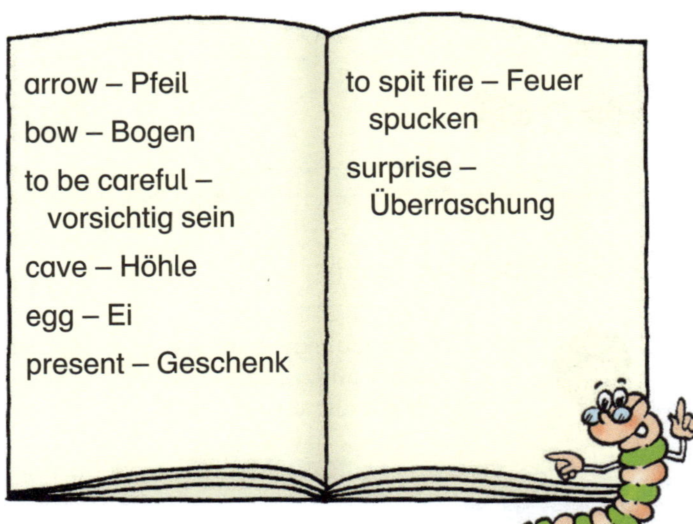

arrow – Pfeil
bow – Bogen
to be careful – vorsichtig sein
cave – Höhle
egg – Ei
present – Geschenk
to spit fire – Feuer spucken
surprise – Überraschung

3. Who is it? Write.

She is my mum's mother. She is my ______________.

Her name is ______________.

He is my mum's father. He is my ______________.

His name is ______________.

Can you guess who it is?

Her name is Milly. She is my ______________.

He is my dad's brother. He is my ______________.

His name is ______________.

She is the daughter of my dad's brother. She is my ______________.

Her name is ______________.

4. Read the words. Write.

br th r

____

mother

____

cousin

____

a n

____

a

____

fatherandgr

____

5. Describe your family.

I've got a mother, a father and a sister. What about you?

I've got ______________.

 6. Read and write.

My best friend is ______________. He has got 2 ______________ and can spit ______________.

My best friend's ______________ is Tom. He is a ______________. 
He has got ______________ hair and brown ______________. 
He is wearing a green ______________ and blue ______________. 
I ______________ him, because he's funny.

My best friend is a ______________. She has got long black ______________ and dark ______________. She is from ______________. I like her because she is ______________.

My ______________ friend is a girl. She ______________ short blond hair and green eyes. She loves to wear ______________ and to read ______________. I like her because we play ______________ together.

dresses boy brown Japan eyes (2x) jeans green legs name like hair best has got T-shirt clever books tennis girl fire

Comic

What a morning!

It's early Sunday morning.

Sally opens the fridge.

Oh no! No milk for hot chocolate. No orange juice, no ham, no eggs, no jam.

No cornflakes, no honey, no bread, no breakfast.

HONEY

BREAD

Sally is sad.

It's not my day today. I'm going back to bed.

Oh Koala, I like hot choco-late and eggs, toast with jam and orange juice for break-fast. But I like you best!

 1. What does Koala bring for breakfast. Read and tick ✓.

For breakfast Koala brings …

☐ hot chocolate
eggs
toast with honey
orange juice

☐ hot chocolate
eggs
toast with jam
apple juice

☐ hot chocolate
eggs
toast with jam
orange juice

Finde das richtige Tablett und kreuze es an.

 2. What do you like for breakfast? Draw and write.

bread breakfast butter cheese cornflakes egg ham honey
jam roll toast drinks apple juice coffee coke hot chocolate
lemonade milk orange juice tea water to eat to drink

3. Find the words. Write and draw lines.

4. Read and colour. Find the matching answer for each question.

What do you have for breakfast?

Do you like milk in your tea?

Can I have the butter, please?

Would you like some cheese?

Pass me the bacon, please.

Here you are.

For breakfast I have toast with ham.

Yes, please.

No, I don't. I like sugar.

Here you are.

Male die Frage und die passende Antwort in derselben Farbe aus.

 5. What do they say? Write the dialogue.

 Betty

 Jack

Wenn du Hilfe brauchst, schaue in Aufgabe 4 nach.

 Frage Betty was sie zum Frühstück isst.

 Sage, dass du zum Frühstück Toast mit Käse isst.

 Frage Jack ob er Milch in seinem Tee mag.

 Verneine.

 Bitte Jack dir den Honig zu reichen.

 Reiche Betty den Honig.

 Comic

The fruit expert

Do melons grow on trees?
Why are bananas curved?
Do pineapples grow on apple trees?
Now I'd like to have a fruit salad.
Me too. But where do we get the fruit from?

No, melons grow on the ground.
Because they grow towards the sun.
No, they grow on the ground, like melons.
We've already got a watermelon, a banana and a pineapple. And in my pouch I've got apples, pears, strawberries, plums, …

 1. Read and circle the correct word.

Bananas are curved / round.

Melons grow on trees / the ground.

Sally has got fruit / lollipops in her pouch.

Pineapples grow on trees / the ground.

Kreise das passende Wort ein, um den Satz zu vervollständigen.

2. Write the name of the trees.

fruit apple banana cherry lemon melon
orange pear pineapple plum strawberry

2. Find the 10 fruit words. Circle and write.

s	t	r	a	w	b	e	r	r	y	l
r	p	i	n	e	a	p	p	l	e	p
o	k	a	d	g	h	o	t	b	p	z
r	p	p	e	a	r	w	r	y	h	l
a	o	f	b	a	n	a	n	a	j	e
n	u	s	e	i	u	w	s	p	m	m
g	k	b	g	a	c	o	b	p	o	o
e	y	p	l	u	m	l	k	l	y	n
t	c	a	h	y	w	e	a	e	d	a
c	h	e	r	r	y	y	l	s	a	b
t	i	p	d	n	z	m	e	l	o	n

Finde die Wörter senkrecht und waagrecht. Kreise sie ein. Schreibe sie dann unten auf.

3. Fill in.

Apples are red, ______ or yellow. They grow on ______.

Cherries are sour or ______. Plums are ______ and have got a stone inside. Bananas are curved because they grow towards the ______. Strawberries are red. They grow on the ______.

______ grow on the ground, too. They are round and big.

Lemons grow on trees. They are ______.

purple	green	sun	melons	trees	sweet	ground	sour

4. Read and write.

Which fruit grow on trees?

______

which = welche

Which fruit grow on the ground?

______

Which fruit are sweet?

______

Which fruit are sour?

______

Which fruit do you like best?

______

Comic

New friends

In the kitchen…

Mummy, what can I do? It's so boring!

Go out and play with your friends, Tom. But be back for dinner.

But nobody has time to play with Tom.

In the street…

Hey, little cat, do you want to be my new friend?

Miaow!

At the playground…

Hello!

Oh, a parrot! Do you want to be my new friend, too?

In the forest…

Hi tortoise. Do you want to be my new friend, too?

In front of Tom's house …

A dog! Do you want to be my new friend, too?

Bow, wow!

I'm back with my friends. Can they have dinner with us?

Yes, sit down.

SALT

Oh, no!

1. Read and answer.

Schau dir nochmal den Comic an und beantworte die Fragen.

Where does Tom find the dog?

What animal does Tom find at the playground?

What colour is the parrot?

How many new friends has Tom got?

Who are Tom's new friends?

pet budgie cat dog fish guinea pig hamster mouse rabbit tortoise ears legs big small fast slow long short brown black grey white

boring – langweilig
dinner – Abendessen
to fly – fliegen
forest – Wald
in front of – vor
kitchen – Küche
to meet – treffen
new – neu
playground – Spielplatz
street – Straße
to swim – schwimmen
time – Zeit
tail – Schwanz
wing – Flügel

 2. Find my pet. Read and circle.

My cat is black and white with green eyes.

My dog is brown and big. It has got short ears.

My parrot is green and yellow. It likes to eat nuts.

My guinea pig is brown and white. It has got long hair.

3. Find the plural. Write.

one dog – two dogs

one fish – three ______

one hamster – two ______

one mouse – three ______

one guinea pig – four ______

one budgie – ten ______

one cat – two ______

Die Mehrzahl von Nomen bildet man, indem man ein -s an das Wort hängt, z. B. 1 dog – 2 dogs. Es gibt aber auch unregelmäßige Nomen: 1 fish – 3 fish; 1 mouse – 2 mice.

4. Write 5 sentences.

Dogs		**water.**
Fish		**milk.**
Hamsters	**drink**	**fly.**
Budgies	**can**	**swim.**
Cats		

______

______

______

______

______

Setze aus den verschiedenen Bestandteilen im Kasten 5 sinnvolle Sätze zusammen und schreibe sie auf.

 Comic

Sally, you are special, too!

Sally is on the farm.
Hello, I'm Tilda the cow. I can give milk. What about you?
I can't give milk.

Hello, I'm Sheila the sheep. I can give wool. What about you?
I can't give wool.

Hello, I'm Henny the hen. I can lay eggs. What about you?
I can't lay eggs.

Sally is sad.

Sally, what's the matter?
I'm sad. I can't give milk, I can't give wool and I can't lay eggs. I can't do anything special.

Miaow!
Oh no. We have to help the little cat.

Thank you Sally.
Sally, maybe you can't give milk, give wool or lay eggs. But you can jump up very high. You are special, too.

1. What can the animals do? Write sentences.

give wool.

give milk.

can

jump high.

lay eggs.

The hen

cat cow dog duck goose – geese hen horse pig sheep – sheep

to help – helfen
to give – geben
high – hoch
to lay eggs – Eier legen
wool – Wolle

 2. Where do the words end? Circle and write.

 3. Which animal is it? Write.

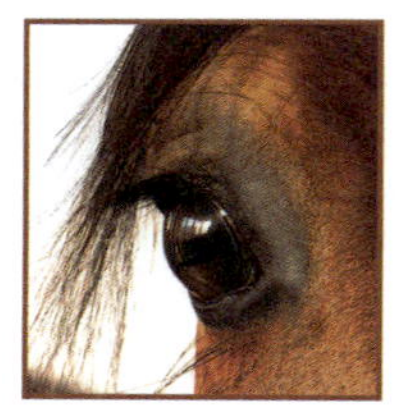

4. Read and fill in.

A day on the farm

Farmer Jonny gets up at 5 o'clock in the __________. He milks the __________. He collects the eggs from the __________. He feeds the __________ and the __________.

Then farmer Jonny brings the cows and the sheep outside so that they can eat the green __________. He makes butter from the __________. For his new warm pullover he takes the __________ from the __________. After a long day farmer Jonny is hungry. He __________ a glass of milk and he __________ bread with ham and eggs. Now Jonny is tired and goes to __________.

geese pigs morning cows bed grass hens sheep drinks milk wool eats

Denke daran, die Mehrzahl von Nomen wird gebildet, indem man ein -s an das Wort anhängt, z.B. 1 hen – 2 hens. Achtung, hier gibt es auch unregelmäßige Nomen: sheep – sheep, goose – geese.

Comic

Dangerous jelly fish

One day, the Millers are having a picnic on the beach.

What a nice day.

In the afternoon the Millers go home. But look at the beach: there is plastic everywhere

Oh no, what a mess!

Here comes a big wave.

Now all the plastic waste is in the sea.

What a yummy little fish.
I'm hungry. I'm going to eat this jelly fish.
Let me help you!
LIFE GUARD
Thank you for saving me!
Don't leave your plastic waste on the beach. Plastic kills our nature!

1. True or false? Tick ✓.

	true	false
The Millers are having a picnic on the beach.	○	○
Plastic bottles and plastic bags are in the sea.	○	○
The fish eats the plastic bag.	○	○
The turtle helps the man.	○	○
The man helps the turtle.	○	○
Plastic is good for our nature.	○	○

beach **fish** **nature** **picnic**

bag – Tüte
bottle – Flasche
dangerous – gefährlich
to help – helfen
hungry – hungrig
jelly fish – Qualle
to kill – umbringen
to leave – zurücklassen
life guard – Rettungsschwimmer
plastic – Plastik
to save – retten
sea – Meer
turtle – Wasserschildkröte
waste – Abfall
wave – Welle
What a mess! – Was für eine Unordnung!
Yummy! – Lecker

2. What do they say? Look and write.

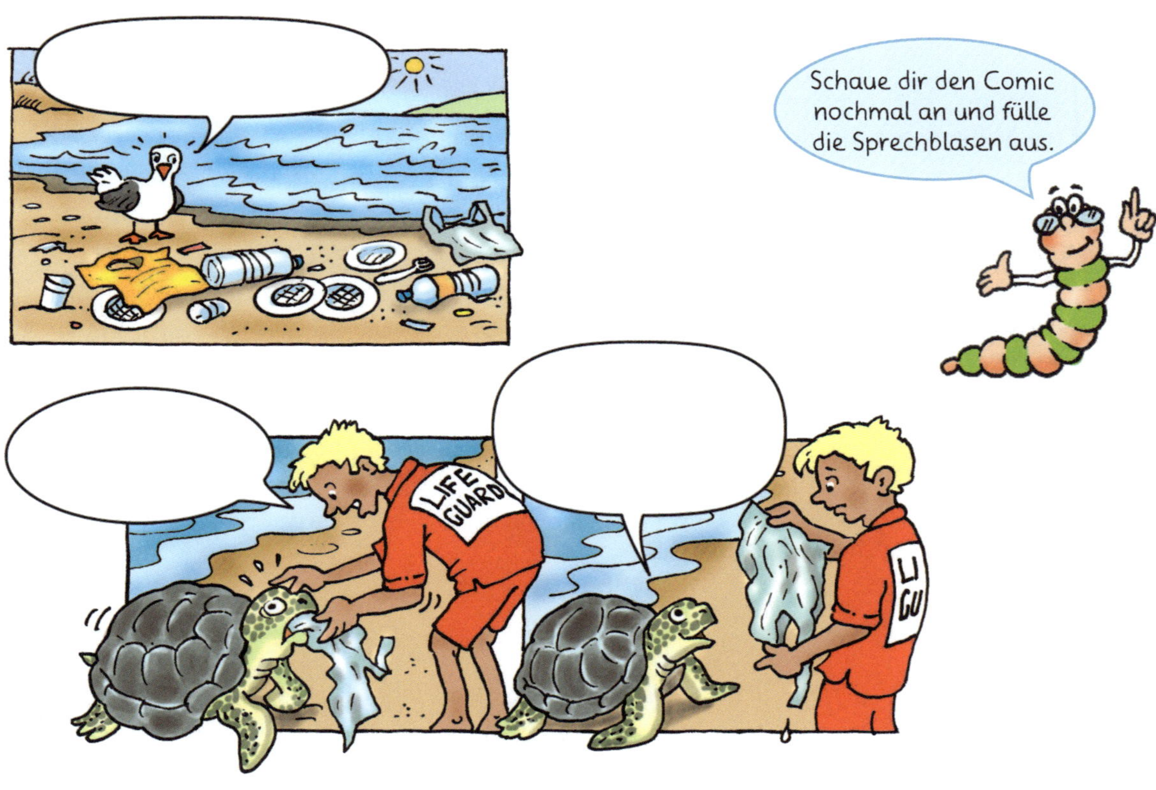

Schaue dir den Comic nochmal an und fülle die Sprechblasen aus.
LIFE GUARD
LI GU

3. What belongs into the sea? Circle.

Was gehört ins Meer? Kreise die passenden Wörter ein.

4. Do the crossword.

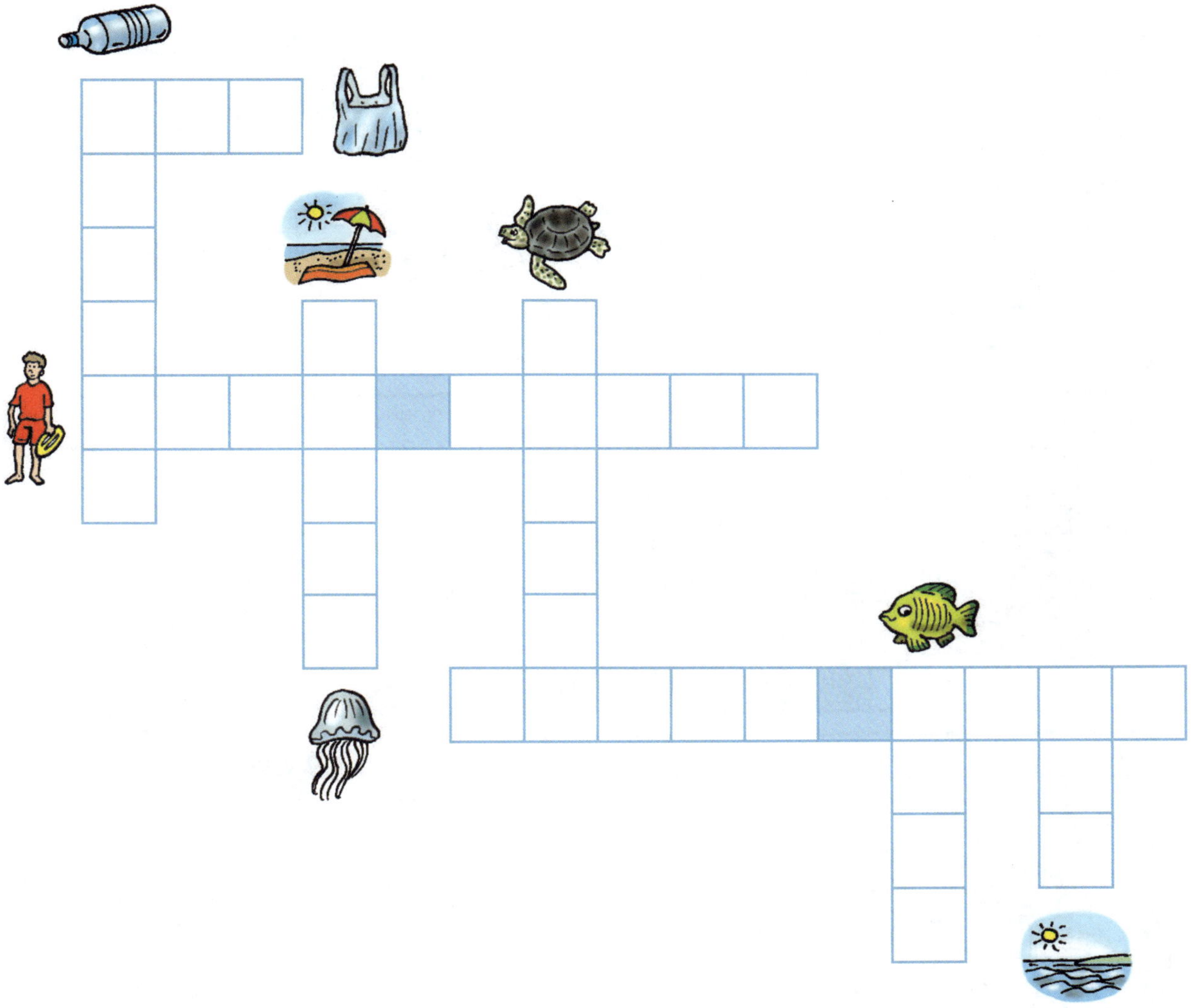

5. Odd one out. Cross out the word that doesn't match.

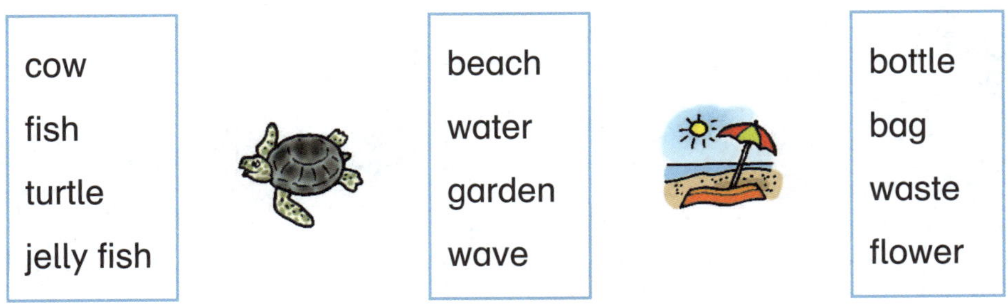

cow	beach	bottle
fish	water	bag
turtle	garden	waste
jelly fish	wave	flower

 Comic

The story of St. George

A long time ago a dangerous dragon attacks the city.

Give me the princess!

Give the princess to the dragon. The dragon is dangerous.

Help us!

Everybody is scared.

The king gives the princess to the dragon.

I'm so sorry. I love you!

Goodbye Father!

George the knight comes along and sees the princess.

What are you doing here?

I'm waiting for the dragon. He wants to kill me.

Oh no, the dragon is coming.

I can kill the dragon for you!

George kills the dragon. The princess is very happy.

Thank you George! Thank you for saving my life. Thank you for saving the city.

The people are very happy and have a big party.

Long live George the knight!

1. Read the comic. Fill in the gaps.

A dangerous ______________ attacks the city. The ______________ gives the princess to the dragon. George the knight sees the ______________. The dragon wants to ______________ the princess. ______________ fights against the dragon. He kills the ______________. The princess and the king are very ______________. They have a big ______________ in the city.

princess	dragon (2x)	king	party	kill	George	happy

Der heilige Georg ist der Schutzpatron von England. Im Union Jack kannst du das rote Georgskreuz erkennen.

Big Ben
Buckingham Palace
double-decker-bus
guard
London Eye
taxi
River Thames
Tower Bridge
Tower of London
Union Jack

to attack – angreifen
city – Stadt
dangerous – gefährlich
dragon – Drache
to fight – kämpfen
to help – helfen
to kill – töten
knight – Ritter
life – Leben
map – Karte
people – Volk
to save – retten
sight – Sehenswürdikgkeiten

3. Find these London sights on the map. Number.

(1) Tower Bridge (2) Buckingham Palace (3) London Eye

(4) Tower of London (5) Big Ben (6) River Thames

UNDERGROUND
BUS STOP
ROUTEMASTER
BUS STOP
UNDERGROUND

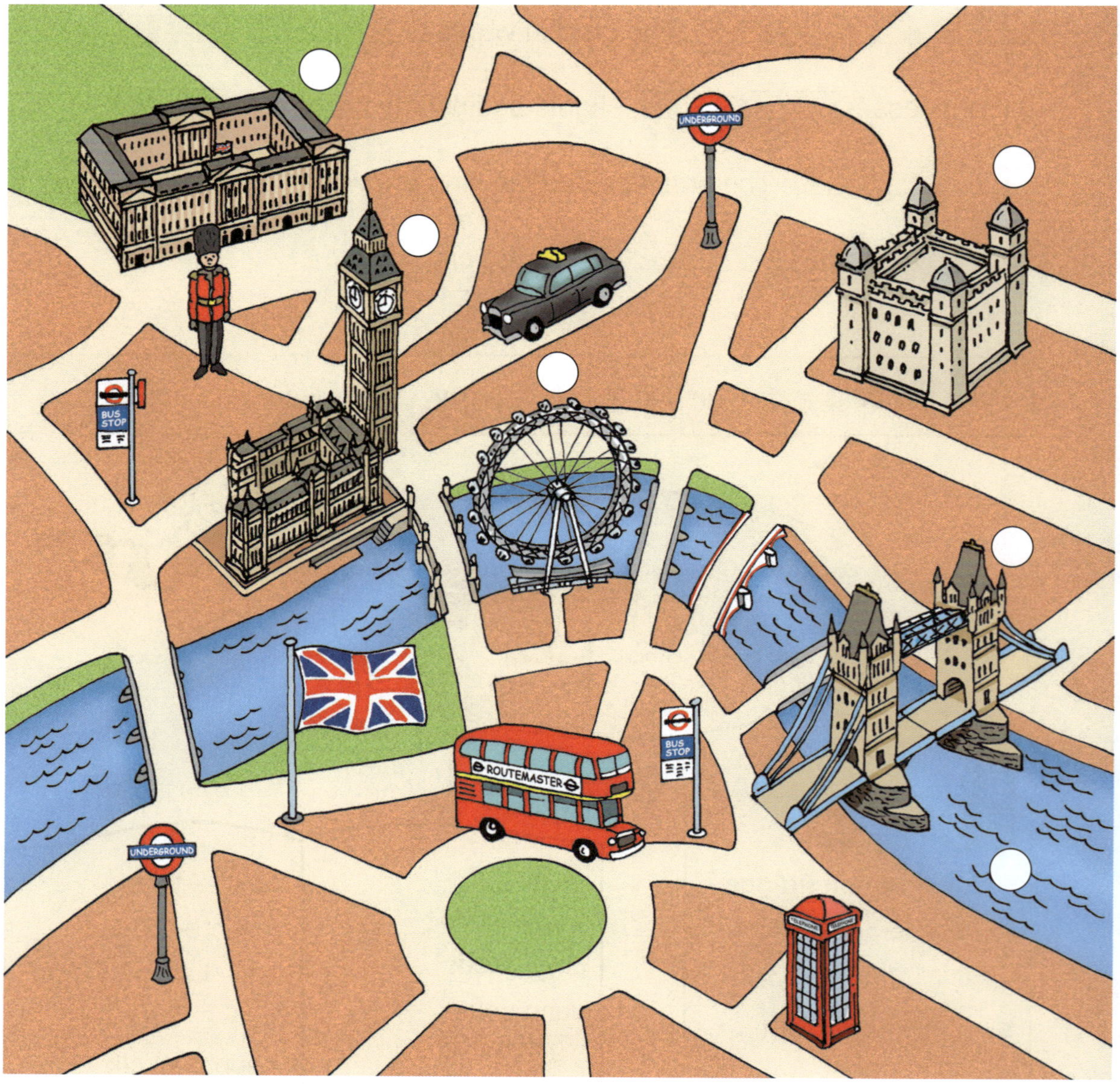

Can you also find the following things on the map? Circle.

a taxi, a double-decker bus, the Union Jack, guard, telephone booth

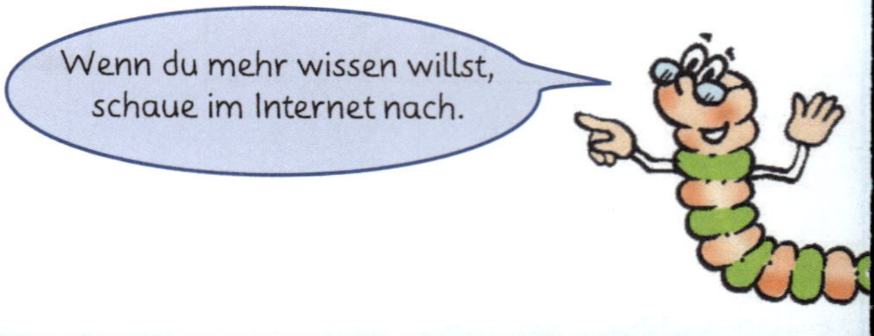

Wenn du mehr wissen willst,
schaue im Internet nach.

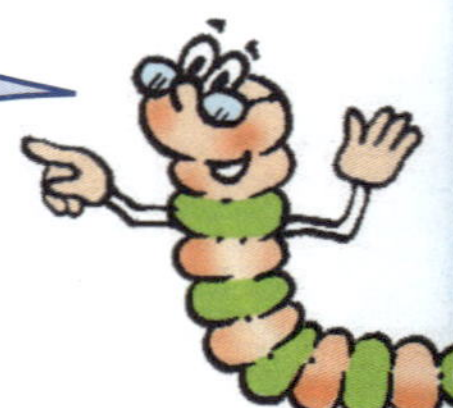